THE LAST MONKS
OF SKELLIG MICHAEL

By Philip Kosloski

CONTENTS

INTRODUCTION

The most fantastic and impossible rock in the world: Skellig Michael...the Skelligs are pinnacled, crocketed, spired, arched, caverned, minaretted; and these gothic extravagances are not curiosities of the islands: they are the islands: there is nothing else. The rest of the cathedral may be under the sea for all I know...An incredible, impossible, mad place...I tell you the thing does not belong to any world that you and I have lived and worked in: it is part of our dream world.

GEORGE BERNARD SHAW

The solitary peaks of Skellig Michael off the coast of County Kerry certainly appear not to belong to this world. They seem to rise out of nowhere from the depths of the sea and possess an aura of mystical energy that enchants all those who approach them.

It was this beauty and ancient spiritual vibrancy that attracted director J.J. Abrams to transplant the island into the Star Wars universe. Executive producer Tommy Harper explained in a short behind-the-scenes video for *The Force Awakens* how "I got an email from Rick Carter [Production Designer of *Star Wars: The Force Awakens*]. He sent this link, and it was Skellig Island. J.J. [Abrams] immediately wrote back and said, 'I love you! This is the best.'"[i]

Martin Joy, supervising location director, explained how they needed "somewhere completely from another time and place" for the new Star Wars trilogy.[ii] When the production team reached Skellig Michael, they were blown away by its beauty and were extremely grateful for the chance to film there. Both Mark Hamill and Daisy Ridley described the experience of filming there as "indescribable" and "unbelievable."[iii]

Filming on Skellig Michael provided an added authenticity to the Star Wars planet of Ahch-To, a place in the fictional universe that was home to the first Jedi Temple and a refuge for character Luke Skywalker. The production team needed a location that possessed an ancient spiritual past to illustrate the origins of the Jedi Order, and they struck gold with Skellig Michael. When visiting the island, New York Times writer Lucinda Hahn wrote about this authenticity, reflecting how she "imagined Luke Skywalker in one of the dank beehive cells, crouching as the monks had centuries before, marooned on the island with his demons."[iv]

A Thousand-Year Spiritual Heritage

While the physical location of Skellig Michael is extremely inspiring, what is even more fascinating is how a group of Irish monks made the island their home over one thousand years ago. Believed to have been founded in the late sixth to early seventh century, the solitary monks lived on the island for a period of six hundred years.

Very few historical records document the life of these monks, but recent archeological research, added to what we already know of early Christian monasticism in Ireland, paints a fairly accurate picture of who these religious monks were and why they left the mainland to establish a monastery on Skellig Michael.

I hope, in the pages of this short book, to give the reader an authentic description of these ancient monks who ultimately inspired the production team of Star Wars. Besides describing the daily life of these spiritual masters, I will detail the amazing symbolism behind every choice they made on the island. Whether it was choosing how to build their cells or how to shave their heads, the monks did everything with the ultimate destiny of Heaven in their minds.

The Warrior Monks of George Lucas

Before we begin delving into the lives of these monks, what's interesting is that the original creator of Star Wars also had in mind Christian monks while inventing the spiritual lineage of the Jedi. While it is true that the Jedi closely resemble samurai warriors of the past and teach others in the Star Wars universe a belief in the Force that is reminiscent of some Buddhist teachings; George Lucas also fashioned the Jedi after the warrior monks of early Christianity.

In early drafts of the Star Wars script, Lucas wrote about a 16-year-old boy who seeks entrance into the "Intersystems Academy to train as a potential Jedi-Templer."[v] Lucas deliberately used the word "Jedi-Templer," in a nod to the warrior religious monks historically known as the "Knights Templar." After these initial drafts, the word Templer was discarded, but Lucas did not drop the idea entirely, referring to the spiritual sages throughout his films as "Jedi Knights."

The Knights Templar, officially known as the Poor Fellow-Soldiers of Christ and the Temple of Solomon, were a Catholic military order established at about the same time the monks on Skellig Michael were leaving the island. The religious group was composed of soldiers sent to the Holy Land during the Crusades to protect pilgrims traveling to the sacred sites of Jesus' passion, death, and resurrection. Saint Bernard of Clairvaux was instrumental in creating a rule for the new religious order, and the Cistercian habit of Saint Bernard provided inspiration for the Templar's clothing.

Eventually, the Knights Templar were disbanded by the Pope and a jealous king sought to annihilate the order. Some believe that this too inspired George Lucas as, "Much like the Great Jedi Purge ordered by Chancellor Palpatine in 'Revenge of the Sith,' France's King Philip IV annihilated the Knights Templar after arresting hundreds of them on October 13, 1307, and subsequently torturing and executing them for heresy."[vi]

The Lord Be With You

Besides having a connection to the Christian monks of the Middle Ages, the Jedi also use a phrase that is intimately tied to the Christian religion. The popular phrase "May the force be with you," is in fact "a variation on the Christian phrase May the Lord be with you and with your spirit—in Latin, Dominus vobiscum et cum Spiritu tuo, which was often written by Saint Paul at the end of his letters."[vii] Producer Gary Kurtz confirmed the phrase was intentionally evocative of the blessing often used in Catholic liturgical ceremonies.[viii]

To even make more connection, the monks on Skellig Michael would have used the phrase "May the Lord be with you" very often in their own liturgy on the island.

In the end, the mysterious monastery atop the jutting rock of Skellig Michael has fascinated the world for centuries and will continue to do so for centuries to come. And whatever authenticity there may be in the Star Wars movies was only made possible by the many sacrifices of the monks who lived there a thousand years ago. In this short book, let's look at their lives and discover who they were and what they can teach us one-thousand years later.

WHY SKELLIG MICHAEL?

Jesus said to him: "If thou wilt be perfect, go sell what thou hast, and give to the poor, and thou shalt have treasure in heaven: and come follow me."

MATTHEW 19:21

Before we can examine the daily life of these ancient monks, we must look at their intentions and mission. We have to ask the simple question, "Why did these men travel in a small boat seven miles off the coast of Ireland to a remote island and establish a monastery, completely separated from the rest of the world?"

Peregrinatio Pro Dei Amore

In the centuries after Saint Patrick established the Christian religion on the island, there grew a religious fervor that took its motto as, *peregrinatio pro Dei amore* — wandering for the love of the Lord. This single phrase inspired numerous holy men and women in Ireland to travel distant places in honor of God.

This idea took various forms during the early years of faith in Ireland, but the desire to get in a boat and sail away from the mainland in search of God remained a common theme. One of the most well-known saints who traveled at this time was Saint Brendan the Navigator. He is known as one of the "Twelve Apostles of Ireland," and numerous legends have become associated with the travels of this adventurous monastic saint.

Throughout his life, Saint Brendan sailed to many distant lands, including Iceland. There is even a story that Brendan made the perilous journey all the way to what is modern-day Florida. However wild that may seem, some scholars believe it could have been possible for Brendan to accomplish that great feat.

Into the Desert

Besides being inspired by the many saints who "wandered for the love of the Lord," the monks who ultimately traveled to Skellig Michael were trying to imitate the Desert Fathers in Egypt who renounced everything and led a life of contemplation in the desert.

The monks in Ireland were very familiar with the *Life of Anthony*, a biography written by Saint Athanasius of Alexandria that described the extreme life of Saint Anthony the Abbot. It was written in 360 and captivated the hearts of the Irish when it was brought to Ireland and copied by the monks in their monasteries.

Furthermore, scholars have recently discovered a tangible link between the Irish Church and Christians in Egypt. In 2006 an Irish worker discovered an amazing find while digging in a bog with his backhoe at Fadden More. He found an intact manuscript from the 9th century and the most significant find was the original leather cover that protected the psalter. The cover was lined with papyrus, a writing material produced from reeds in the Mediterranean. Some scholars argue that this discovery further cements the unique connection between these two early Christian communities.

Saint Athanasius describes Saint Anthony as a man who was inspired by various Gospel passages to imitate the disciples of Jesus and renounce everything for the love of God.

"After the death of his father and mother [Saint Anthony] was left alone with one little sister: his age was about eighteen or twenty, and on him the care both of home and sister rested. Now it was not six months after the death of his parents, and going according to custom into the Lord's House, he communed with himself and reflected as he walked how the Apostles [Matthew 4:20] left all and followed the Saviour; and how they in the Acts [Acts 4:35] sold their possessions and brought and laid them at the Apostles' feet for distribution to the needy, and what and how great a hope was laid up for them in heaven. Pondering over these things he entered the church, and it happened the Gospel was being read, and he heard the Lord saying to the rich man [Matthew 19:21], 'If you would be perfect, go and sell what you have and give to the poor; and come follow Me and you shall have treasure in heaven.' Anthony, as though God had put him in mind of the Saints, and the passage had been read on his account, went out immediately from the church, and gave the possessions of his forefathers to the villagers—they were three hundred acres, productive and very fair—that they should be no more a clog upon himself and his sister. And all the rest that was movable he sold, and having got together much money he gave it to the poor, reserving a little however for his sister's sake."

After giving himself entirely to God, Anthony sought out a local hermit for spiritual wisdom and eventually chose to live out the rest of his life in the desert.

"Now there was then in the next village an old man who had lived the life of a hermit from his youth up. Anthony, after he had seen this man, imitated him in piety. And at first he began to abide in places outside the village: then if he heard of a good man anywhere, like the prudent bee, he went forth and sought him, nor turned back to his own palace until he had seen him; and he returned, having got from the good man as it were supplies for his journey in the way of virtue...he went forth still more eagerly bent on the service of God and...asked [the old man] to dwell with him in the desert. But when the other declined on account of his great age, and because as yet there was no such custom, Anthony himself set off immediately to the mountain."

Essentially, Anthony desired to imitate the example of Jesus, who spent forty days in the desert in prayer and freely chose to spend his life in a remote and harsh location for the glory of God.

Green Martyrdom

Along with this desire to go into the desert and contemplate God, the monks of Ireland held on to the concept of a "green martyrdom." The Catholic Church has always taught about the possibility of a "red martyrdom," where one imitates Jesus' sacrifice on the cross by dying for the sake of the Gospel. Additionally, there was the belief that if a person wasn't called to a red martyrdom, they could participate in the same sacrifice with a "white martyrdom," where someone might endure ridicule for belief in the Gospel, but not suffer death.

Early on, especially in Ireland, there developed a third martyrdom called, "green martyrdom." An ancient Irish homily, written around the end of the seventh century, gives a perfect summary of this type of martyrdom.

"Now there are three kinds of martyrdom, which are accounted as a cross to a man, to wit: white martyrdom, green and red martyrdom. White martyrdom consists in a man's abandoning everything he loves for God's sake, though he suffer fasting or labor thereat. Green martyrdom consists in this, that by means of fasting and labor he frees himself from his evil desires, or suffers toil in penance and repentance."

The Irish took hold of this type of martyrdom and, not surprisingly, sought out remote "green" places to live out this green martyrdom. They wanted to be as severe as they could in fasting and penance, and so they preferred the harshest and remote places possible.

A Soldier in Christ's Army

Along with these ideas, the Irish monks gladly accepted the thought that they were "soldiers of Christ" (*miles Christi*). This came from another Desert Father, Saint John Cassian, whose writings greatly influenced Ireland.

In his *Institutes*, Cassian constantly refers to the monk devoted to God as a soldier.

"A monk, then, as a soldier of Christ ever ready for battle..."

"Clad, therefore, in these vestments, the soldier of Christ..."

"Our foe is shut up within ourselves: an internal warfare is daily waged by us: and if we are victorious in this, all external things will be made weak, and everything will be made peaceful and subdued for the soldier of Christ."

The imagery used by Cassian is straight from the letters of Saint Paul, who urged the community of Ephesus to "put on the armor of God."

"[B]e strengthened in the Lord, and in the might of his power. Put you on the armor of God, that you may be able to stand against the deceits of the devil. For our wrestling is not against flesh and blood; but against principalities and power, against the rulers of the world of this darkness, against the spirits of wickedness in the high places. Therefore take unto you the armor of God, that you may be able to resist in the evil day, and to stand in all things perfect. Stand therefore, having your loins girt about with truth, and having on the breastplate of justice, And your feet shod with the preparation of the gospel of peace: In all things taking the shield of faith, wherewith you may be able to extinguish all the fiery darts of the most wicked one. And take unto you the helmet of salvation, and the sword of the Spirit (which is the word of God). By all prayer and supplication praying at all times in the spirit; and in the same watching with all instance and supplication for all the saints." (Ephesians 6:10-18)

Saint Patrick also brought this analogy to the Irish with his lorica or "Breastplate" prayer. The prayer is meant to be a protection against the dark spiritual forces of this world and calls upon "God's Shield to shelter me."

Irishmen, in particular, held fast to this concept, as they retained a great desire to fight even after being converted to Christianity. The thought of putting on the "armor of God" gave them the ability to harness that desire for combat and instead of joining a military army, enlisted in a spiritual army poised to defeat the power of the Evil One.

Trained for Spiritual Battle at an Early Age

As the early monasteries of Ireland flourished, families from all over the country sought to send their children to be educated and possibly remain as a monk or nun. They were accepted at the monastery around age seven and stayed there until age seventeen. At that point in the child's education, the elders of the monastery would discern if they were to stay forever dedicated to God or depart the cloister and start a family.

This intense spiritual training at an early age prepared the monks for lifelong service in the Church. It was only after this rigorous "Jedi Academy" type of training that any monk could depart from his monastery to become a secluded hermit and do spiritual battle in the desert.

At the Edge of the World

All of this builds up to the man responsible for founding the monastery on Skellig Michael: Saint Fionán (also known as Saint Finnian). What can be confusing is that there are many similar names in the Irish collection of saints and it is easy to attribute the establishment of other monasteries to this particular saint. However, the Saint Fionán who embarked on a journey to the "Great Skellig" off the coast of County Kerry, did not accomplish any of these great deeds.

It is believed that Saint Fionán set out on his quest for a "green desert" near the end of the sixth century after spending several years praying and studying at a local monastery on the mainland. Being the abbot of a new community, he would have been a priest with a reputation of holiness that preceded his adventure to the edge of the known world.

At the time this breaking away was a common practice in Irish monasteries, with many monks across the country asking for permission to become a hermit in the most remote areas possible. They did this in imitation of the Desert Fathers, whom they greatly admired.

Saint Fionán set out, in imitation of the Apostles, with twelve men who were filled with the same zeal for God. They reached the Great Skellig by traveling on a small boat, not even sure that they would make it to their destination. Upon arrival, the close-knit group of monks set to work and over the next 600 years, became a foundation for a monastery that would be known for its holiness and extreme way of life.

Blind Man's Cove

Landing Place

Blue Cove

Cross

Cross

Needles Eye

Burial Ground

Christ's Valley

Cross

Light Ho.

Cross

Cross Cove

Seal Cove

Blue Man's Rock

Lower Light Ho.

Scale 12 in to a Mile.

GREAT SKELLIG ROCK.

SCELIG MHICHIL, ST. MICHAEL'S ROCK, CO. KERRY.

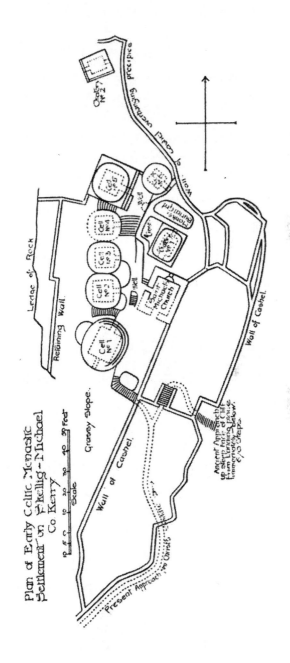

Plan of Early Celtic Monastic
Settlement on Skellig-Michael
Co Kerry

Scale

0 5 10 20 30 40 50 Feet

Oratory Nº 2?

Wall of Cashel

Grassy Slope.

Ledge of Rock

Retaining Wall.

Cell Nº 1

Cell Nº 2

Cell Nº 3

Cell Nº 4

Cell Nº 5

Cell Nº 6

Well

Oratory Nº 1

Monks' Burial Ground

Well

Wall of Cashel.

St. Michael's Church

Wall of Cashel

Present Approach via Christ's Saddle

Ancient Approach up steep face of Cliff from Landing Place immediately below. c/o Steps

27

THE HIVE OF SPIRITUAL NOURISHMENT

The bee is more honored than other animals, not because it labors, but because it labors for others.

SAINT JOHN CHRYSOSTOM

After arriving on Skellig, the monks had to create a dwelling that was both functional and spiritual. Over the centuries, they built a style of buildings that can be found in many places in Ireland, the "beehive" hut, which is also known as a "clochán." The huts were built with the local rocks available to them and were created to shield the monks from the harsh weather atop the rock.

Archeological evidence has identified the remains of six beehive cells, two oratories, two wells, five burial grounds, several rough crosses, and a small church that was dedicated to Saint Michael the Archangel. Additionally, there were several open-air *leachta,* small rectangular structures of stone similar to an altar that are believed to have been used for Mass and other liturgies. The cells typically housed 2-3 monks at a time and were mainly used as sleeping quarters. It is believed that no more than 12-13 monks lived on the island at one time.

The cells were designed with a distinct architecture that resembles an ancient artificial beehive called a *skep*, which was essentially a domed woven basket that was kept over the bees. Bees were revered both in pagan cultures as well as in Christianity. They were seen as symbols of wisdom and the bees' ordered life in the hive provided ample meditation for the monastic monks.

Pope Pius XII gave an address in 1948 to apiarists assembled in Rome, drawing on the wisdom of the early Church Fathers, and provides an excellent summary of the spiritual lessons that were taught to the monks concerning bees.

"Bees are models of social life and activity, in which each class has its duty to perform and performs it exactly—one is almost tempted to say conscientiously—without envy, without rivalry, in the order and position assigned to each, with care and love. Even the most inexperienced observer of bee culture admires the delicacy and perfection of this work. Unlike the butterfly which flits from flower to flower out of pure caprice; unlike the wasp and the hornet, brutal aggressors, who seem intent on doing only harm with no benefit for anyone, the bee pierces to the very depths of the flower's calix diligently, adroitly, and so delicately, that once its precious treasure has been gathered, it gently leaves the flowers without having injured in the least the light texture of their garments or caused a single one of their petals the loss of its immaculate freshness..

Then, loaded down with sweet-scented nectar, pollen, and propolis, without capricious gyrations, without lazy delays, swift as an arrow, with precise, unerring, certain flight, it returns to the hive, where valorous work goes on intensely to process the riches so carefully garnered, to produce the wax and the honey.

Ah, if men could and would listen to the lesson of the bees: if each one knew how to do his daily duty with order and love at the post assigned to him by Providence...Working like bees with order and peace, men would learn to enjoy and have others enjoy the fruit of their labors, the honey and the sweetness and the light in this life here below."[ix]

Beekeeping was very common in Ireland at that time and was an essential part of monastery life. Beeswax candles were used in the many liturgical ceremonies of the monks and were always in high demand. This too had its own spiritual significance, as "The pure wax extracted by bees from flowers symbolizes the pure flesh of Christ received from His Virgin Mother, the wick signifies the soul of Christ, and the flame represents His divinity."[x]

While the monks on Skellig Michael weren't able to maintain a hive of bees on their small island, they would have been familiar with beekeeping before leaving a monastery on the mainland to embrace their call to the desert life of Skellig.

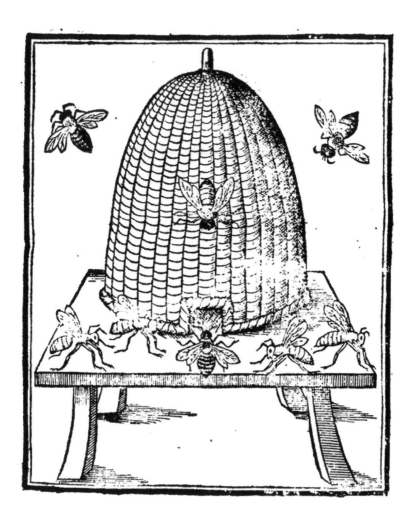

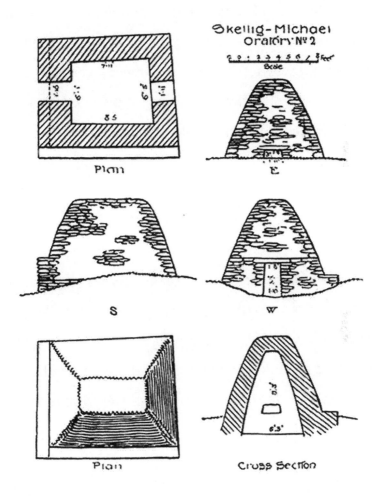

Skellig-Michael
Oratory Nº 2

Scale

Plan

E

S

W

Plan

Cross Section

Pilgrims on a Journey

The central focus of the community, where the "bees" received their nourishment, would have been the various places set apart for divine worship. This included two oratories, several open-air *leachta,* and a small church dedicated to Saint Michael that was built around the eleventh century.

These buildings were not built in the same way as the beehive cells and the ceilings of these structures resembled an inverted boat. Again, this was intentional, evoking a sense of pilgrimage present in Christian belief. Additionally, these structures dedicated to prayer possessed a single window located at the East end of the building. It is believed these monks were following an "ancient custom...to pray facing East, toward the Orient from on high...[and] the ecclesiastical building [was] turned into a 'ship' (nave=*navis*) voyaging towards the East."[xi] The direction of east, besides being the location of the rising sun, has always been associated with new life and it is believed that Jesus will come again at the end of time from the East to create a new heavens and a new earth.

The church building has also been traditionally "compared to an ark, as a place of refuge from the chaos of the churning waters. A nave provides similar protection from the sin of the world, while leading its members on a journey of pilgrimage to heaven."[xii]

With all of these ideas in mind, the monks of Skellig Michael made certain that their places of worship faced east and that the buildings they constructed reminded them of the pilgrimage they were all on as a community.

Saint Michael the Archangel - Slayer of Dragons

At the very latest, it was not until 1044 that the *Sceilig* Island (which simply means "rock in the sea") was referred to as *Sceilig Mhichíl* (Skellig Michael), in honor of the dedication of a church on the island to Saint Michael the Archangel. During this period, several other high places and remote islands were named after Saint

Michael, such as Mont Saint-Michel in France and St. Michael's Mount in England.

This may have been due, in part, to a scriptural reference to Saint Michael in the book of Revelation. In it, Saint Michael casts down the "great dragon" (Satan) from the heights of Heaven and banishes him forever.

"And there was seen another sign in heaven: and behold a great red dragon, having seven heads, and ten horns: and on his head seven diadems...And there was a great battle in heaven, Michael and his angels fought with the dragon, and the dragon fought and his angels...And that great dragon was cast out, that old serpent, who is called the devil and Satan, who seduceth the whole world; and he was cast unto the earth, and his angels were thrown down with him...And I heard a loud voice in heaven, saying: Now is come salvation, and strength, and the kingdom of our God, and the power of his Christ: because the accuser of our brethren is cast forth, who accused them before our God day and night. And they overcame him by the blood of the Lamb, and by the word of the testimony, and they loved not their lives unto death." (Revelation 12:1-11)

Another reason behind the naming of Skellig Michael could be its association with a possible apparition of the archangel on the island.

According to tradition (recorded by Irish monks in the manuscript *Libellus de Fundacione Ecclesie Consecrati Petri*), Saint Patrick was having a difficult time expelling the last demonic creatures from the land and needed some heavenly aid. He was able to drive the beasts to the south-western edge of Ireland and as he stretched out his hand a great heavenly host of angels appeared, with Saint Michael in the lead. This "High King of the Angels" (*Adrigh na Aaingeal*) was visible to Saint Patrick standing on a pinnacle of rock out in the middle of the sea. After Saint Michael cast out the last of the demons and serpents from Ireland he left his shield behind on the Great Skellig.

Furthermore, when the monastery was established on the island, the monks passed down a story regarding a regular visit from Saint Michael to replenish their supply of wine for the celebration of Mass. Below is a retelling of the story by Giraldus Cambrensis, a royal clerk who traveled to Ireland in the 12th century.

"In the southern part of Munster, in the neighborhood of Cork, there is an island with a church dedicated to St. Michael, famed for its orthodox sanctity from very ancient times. There is a stone outside the porch of this church, on the right hand, and partly fixed in the wall, with a hollow in its surface, which, every morning, through the merits of the saint to whom the church is dedicated, is filled with as much wine as will conveniently suffice for the service of the Masses on the day ensuing, according to the number of priests there who have to celebrate them."

In the end, this type of imagery fit well within the Irish monks' spirituality of putting on the "armor of

God" and being a "solider in Christ's army." They saw themselves as great spiritual warriors engaged in the same battle against Satan and so it was not a very difficult choice to name the island (and church) after Saint Michael, the Dragon Slayer.

Worker Bees

Within the community, there was a natural division of labor based on experience and age. Everyone had to work hard to ensure the success of their spiritual foundation, and so each monk was given specific tasks.

An abbot led the community of monks, often called "Abba," in reference to the Aramaic word for "father." This monk was typically older than everyone else, highly regarded for his holiness, and a priestly member of the ordained clergy. It was his responsibility to assign tasks and ensure the spiritual and physical well-being of his monks.

The abbot would also be responsible for admitting new members into the small community.

Since travel was difficult to Skellig Michael, the abbot would make an instant decision when a new monk arrived. He was either allowed to remain and follow the rules of the community, or sent back on the boat he came on.

Additionally, the abbot had the authority to confer various "minor orders" to his monks, such as porter, lector, exorcist, and acolyte. These offices were typically only exercised in the liturgy and specified roles that these monks could now participate in. Ordination to the priesthood required the participation of a local bishop and was often reserved for a small number of monks in the monastery.

Monastic Attire

The monks at Skellig Michael tried to imitate, as much as possible, the Desert Fathers. This even went so far as the type of clothing they wore on the island. It is believed the monks wore a rough gray tunic underneath a hooded cloak that protected them from the elements. They likely did not wear any sandals, unless traveling away from the Skellig.

The clothing was simple and poor, representing how they surrendered everything to God. However, whenever the priest celebrated the sacrifice of the Mass, he would put on a large poncho-like garment called a *casula* (chasuble) that covered his ordinary clothing and symbolized his role as "another Christ" in the liturgy. This vestment developed from the normal Roman attire of a farmer that became associated with Christians in the third century. These were rather simple at first, but by the early Middle Ages became more elaborate and decorative. Underneath the *casula* was a white linen garment with sleeves worn over the tunic called an *alb*, recalling the purity of their baptism.

In addition to the *casula*, there was also a thin strip of material known as a stole worn over the neck and a short linen cloth called an *amice* worn to protect the shoulders and neck from the ornamented *casula*; both vestments were worn beneath the *casula*. Over the years, the *amice* became associated symbolically as a helmet worn for spiritual battle, as can be seen in the ancient vesting prayer, *Impone, Domine, capiti meo galeam salutis, ad expugnandos diabolicos incursus* (Place upon me, O Lord, the helmet of salvation, that I may overcome the assaults of the devil).

Lastly, the Irish monks after the Synod of Whitby in 664 shaved their heads according to the Roman tonsure, leaving a circle of hair around the crown of their heads. This ritual shaving was always done when a man was admitted into the community and symbolized his need to renounce his former life and embrace the new life of the monastery. It was also said to represent the crown of thorns that was placed on the head of Jesus.

What they built and what they wore was all directed towards their daily life and their ultimate goal of Heaven. We will now look at their daily *horarium* and discover the beauty, silence and prayer of the monks on Skellig Michael.

A DAY IN THE LIFE OF A SPIRITUAL WARRIOR

The aim of every monk and the perfection of his heart tends to continual and unbroken perseverance in prayer.

SAINT JOHN CASSIAN

Historically, Jews prayed at fixed intervals throughout the day. King David, who is believed to have written the Psalms, proclaims,

"Evening and morning and at noon
I will speak and declare:
and he shall hear my voice." (Psalm 54:18[55:17])

The prophet Daniel was also shown to have a specific set of times for prayer.

"When Daniel knew that the document had been signed, he went to his house where he had windows in his upper chamber open toward Jerusalem; and he got down upon his knees three times a day and prayed and gave thanks before his God, as he had done previously." (Daniel 6:10)

The Jewish people began a tradition of praying three times a day: morning, afternoon and evening. This developed into a program of praying the Psalms, as these scripture passages expressed the many desires of the human heart. Jesus is recorded praying the Psalms on multiple occasions, most famously the words of Psalm 21[22] ("My God, my God, why hast thou forsaken me?").

Since most Christians converted from Judaism in the decades after Christ's death, they continued the Jewish tradition of praying the Psalms. This type of prayer was maintained as the Church grew and it is recorded, "Throughout the Church, in Palestine, Antioch, Constantinople and Africa, Christians gathered in their churches twice each day to pray the psalms. Daily they assembled for 'morning and evening hymns.'"[xiii]

The early monasteries, especially those of Egypt, took hold of this ancient tradition and inspired by the word of Saint Paul to "pray without ceasing," developed a total of seven times during the day to stop and pray. In imitation of these early monasteries, the Irish monks held fast to the following hours of prayer: Prime (6 a.m.), Terce (9 a.m.), Sext (noon), None (3 p.m.), Vespers (6 p.m.), Nocturns (midnight), and Matins (3 a.m.).

During these hours of prayer, the monks chanted three Psalms and listened to a reading from either the Old Testament or the New Testament. The monks developed a cycle where they chanted all 150 Psalms in Latin every few days, distributed between all the hours. This they did by memory, being one of the first requirements of the monastery. The other readings from scripture, however, would have been read from manuscripts that were copied by the monks.

This regimen of prayer (typically called a *horarium*), added to the monks green martyrdom and provided a daily opportunity for sacrifice. It also meant that their daily work was constantly being interrupted for prayer, reminding the monks of their primary duty as spiritual warriors.

Pray Without Ceasing

In addition to this daily *horarium*, the monks further responded to the call of Saint Paul to "pray without ceasing," by reciting a prayer found in one of the Psalms and highlighted by Saint John Cassian. He wrote in his *Conferences*, "we must give you also the form of this spiritual contemplation, on which you may always fix your gaze with the utmost steadiness, and both learn to consider it to your profit in unbroken continuance, and also manage by the practice of it and by meditation to climb to a still loftier insight. This formula then shall be proposed to you of this system, which you want, and of prayer, which every monk in his progress towards continual recollection of God, is accustomed to ponder, ceaselessly revolving it in his heart, having got rid of all kinds of other thoughts; for he cannot possibly keep his hold over it unless he has freed himself from all bodily cares and anxieties. And as this was delivered to us by a few of those who were left of the oldest fathers, so it is only divulged by us to a very few and to those who are really keen. And so for keeping up continual recollection of God this pious formula is to be ever set before you. O God, make speed to save me: O Lord, make haste to help me, for this verse has not unreasonably been picked out from the whole of Scripture for this purpose."

The prayer comes from Psalm 69[70] and traditionally it was prayed while breathing in and out, making it a part of a monk's very breath. This allowed a monk to remain in a constant state of contemplation calling upon God at every moment of the day. It can also be translated as, "O God, come to my assistance, O Lord, make haste to help me," and is currently part of the Church's *Liturgy of the Hours* that monks, priests, and lay people continue to pray. One could compare it in style to the type of prayer that the character Chirrut Îmwe prays in *Rogue One: A Star Wars Story* ("I am one with the Force. The Force is with me").

The Source and Summit of a Monk's Life

Each morning after the celebration of Terce, the monastic community would participate in the Holy Sacrifice of the Mass, the re-presentation of the Last Supper. At first, Mass was only celebrated on Sundays and special feast days, but it soon became the norm to celebrate Mass every day.

Mass for the Irish monks was a central part of their spirituality and became the backbone of the community. It was within the context of the Mass that the monks would receive the very Body, Blood, Soul and Divinity of Jesus Christ, truly present under the appearances of bread and wine.

This belief that the bread and wine were transformed into Jesus himself was held fast by the early Christians. Saint John Chrysostom of the fifth century proclaimed in an early homily, "It is not the power of man which makes what is put before us the Body and Blood of Christ, but the power of Christ Himself who was crucified for us. The priest standing there in the place of Christ says these words but their power and grace are from God. 'This is My Body,' he says, and these words transform what lies before him." Saint Cyril of Alexandria also attests to this firm belief in a commentary on the Gospel of Matthew in the fifth century, "Christ said indicating (the bread and wine): 'This is My Body,' and 'This is My Blood,' in order that you might not judge what you see to be a mere figure. The offerings, by the hidden power of God Almighty, are changed into Christ's Body and Blood, and by receiving these we come to share in the life-giving and sanctifying efficacy of Christ." Jesus himself also confirmed this belief when he proclaimed in the Gospel of John, "Amen, amen I say unto you: Except you eat the flesh of the Son of man, and drink his blood, you shall not have life in you. He that eateth my flesh, and drinketh my blood, hath everlasting life: and I will raise him up in the last day" (John 6:54-55).

On account of this mystical reality, the monks on Skellig Michael took the celebration of Mass seriously.

It was the focal point of each day and sustained them spirituality on the remote island. The Mass provided that sacred opportunity to become one with Christ in a special way. It was a daily miracle, and the strength they received to work and pray atop the lonely peak flowed from the Mass; without which they may not have lasted very long.

To celebrate the Mass worthily, bread and wine had to be brought in from the mainland every few months. This kept the monks in contact with the wider world as they did not have the resources on the island to maintain the constant supply of bread and wine that they needed. They likely also had to rely on other monasteries for beeswax candles, another basic requirement for the celebration of Mass.

Self-Denial
Again, in imitation of the Desert Fathers of Egypt, the Irish monks were well known for their asceticism and commitment to daily mortification and penance. They took the call to a green martyrdom

seriously and desired to willingly take up sacrifices that would unite them to Jesus' suffering on the cross.

Fasting was one of the principal ways for the monks to keep their sinful inclinations at bay. This was especially true during Lent, when they would only eat every few days. Food was already scarce on the island, consisting of a diet of fish, birds, eggs, and possibly seal, besides what they were able to trade for on the mainland. Food was used for basic survival, keeping their mortal bodies alive, so that they could focus entirely on the spiritual life.

Penance and daily mortification were also a central part of the monks' lives. They would atone for their personal and communal sins by participating in extreme penance. One such example of the practice is known as *crosfigel* (cross-vigil) where a monk stood, knelt or laid down while holding out his hands in a cruciform manner. It was practiced either as a personal method of mortification or as a penance imposed for sin. There is a story about the Irish monk, Saint Kevin of

Glendalough, who practiced the *crosfigel* so long that a bird built a nest in one of his hands.

Besides these methods of self-denial was the ongoing task of building the various structures of the monastery on Skellig Michael. This arduous work of carving out stones to be used for staircases, cells, water cisterns and oratories was maintained by many generations of monks on the island. The labor was intense with access to only the most basic tools at that time. The work itself was a form of mortification and helped strengthen their bodies as well as their souls.

Protectors of Christian Culture

By the 5th century, Rome was losing power and influence in Europe. The Empire was already split and the Roman military of the West was growing weaker in power each day. Barbarian tribes were not afraid of pressing forward into the heart of the Empire and the Romans were relatively useless to stop any advancement.

In 476 the barbarian tribes won the day, sacking Rome, and the Empire's former glory ceased to exist. Furthermore, these new leaders were not fond of Roman ways and sought to destroy anything associated with the classical world. In particular, the classical way of education was almost obliterated and those who now inhabited Western Europe were more concerned about survival than enriching a flourishing culture.

However, one place remained untouched by the barbarian influence: Ireland. Preserved from the upheaval of Europe, Ireland was isolated enough that they were able to keep to themselves. This isolation proved to be a good thing as Saint Patrick laid a strong foundation of Christianity and Western Culture in Ireland as Rome was crumbling.

The monks who lived on Skellig Michael similarly played a vital role in the preservation of Christian culture. While Europe was in chaos, the monks were busy preserving Christian faith and culture through art, literature and education. They were masters of Latin and Greek culture and maintained it through the copying of manuscripts and the passing on of knowledge in their monastic schools. While Skellig Michael did not have a large school on the island, it did have a small library where they kept alive the flame of Western culture and passed it on to the generations of monks who came after them.

In the end, everything that the monks did on Skellig Michael was directed towards their ultimate destination of Heaven. They saw their lives on earth as temporary, a passing shadow that would eventually give way to the light of eternity.

THE LAST MONKS OF SKELLIG MICHAEL AND THEIR LEGACY

The monastic life is a signpost pointing to a journey and quest, a reminder to the entire People of God of the primary and ultimate meaning of the Christian life.

POPE FRANCIS

By the twelfth century, monastic communities in the Catholic Church were beginning to change, and with the rise of the Orders of Saint Benedict, Saint Bruno and the Canons Regular of Saint Augustine, an emphasis was placed on a more centralized administration of monasteries. At the same time, bishops became more powerful in places like Ireland and began to hold more authority over the monasteries in their region.

It is likely that these factors, along with a sudden deterioration of weather on Skellig Michael, forced the monks to leave their beloved desert at the edge of the world. Being completely isolated from the rest of the Church was no longer an option, and so the monks reluctantly made the decision to move their small community across the bay. They established a traditional monastery at Ballinskelligs but kept a protective eye on Skellig Michael for several centuries.

It is believed that the monks would occasionally use the island as a place of retreat as well as assist any pilgrims who desired to set foot on it to fulfill a penance. The monks who once closely followed the example of the Desert Fathers conceded their spiritual heritage and became associated with the Canons Regular of Saint Augustine, which was more closely connected to the European style of monasticism and much less rigorous. However, they maintained their devotion to Saint Michael the Archangel and named their new priory in his honor.

This new foundation lasted until the dissolution of the monasteries that began with Henry VIII and continued through the reign of Elizabeth I. The monastery at Ballinskelligs was consequently abandoned in 1578, and Skellig Michael was transferred into to secular hands, and to this day is currently being looked after by the Irish government.

Legacy

The monks and their foreign way of life have much to teach us one-thousand years later. Their dedication to a harsh life of prayer, penance, and spiritual warfare reminds us there is more to this world than meets the eye. There is a spiritual battle going on, and we are in the midst of it, whether we realize it or not. Pope Francis once said in a homily, "The devil is here…even in the 21st century! And we mustn't be naïve, right? We must learn from the Gospel on how to fight against Satan."[xiv]

Pope John Paul II also brought this reality to light when visiting a shrine dedicated to Saint Michael the Archangel.

"This battle against the devil which characterizes the Archangel Michael is still going on, because the devil is still alive and at work in the world. In fact, the evil that is in it, the disorder we see in society, the infidelity of man, the interior fragmentation of which he is a victim, are not merely the consequences of original sin, but also the effect of the dark and infesting activity of Satan, of this saboteur of man's moral equilibrium."[xv]

The monks journeyed to Skellig Michael with full knowledge that for the rest of their lives, they would be battling against the "Dark Side" of this world. They knew it would not be an easy fight and freely chose a life of self-denial, so they could defeat the power of Satan and clear the path to Eternal Life.

How to Fight

We must not stand idly by, thinking that we are somehow immune from this spiritual battle. For those baptized in the Catholic Church, the spiritual gauntlet was thrown at the very beginning of life. At baptism, the Godparents declared war in the baptismal promises.

Do you reject Satan? (I do)

And all his works? (I do)

And all his empty promises? (I do)

This proclamation has not gone unnoticed, and for the remainder of a Christian's life on earth, Satan is there trying to lead the soul further and further away from the loving embrace of God. As a consequence, Christians need to be vigilant and actively fight against such an assault, or else be taken further and further into despair and self-destruction.

What can we do to fight back? The monks on Skellig Michael point us in the right direction. We must discover ways in our own lives to practice self-denial, pray "without ceasing," and wield the "sword of the spirit" boldly. We must find our own "green martyrdom," and seek it out for the benefit of our eternal soul. This won't be easy, but with the help of God, all things are possible.

For example, we could imitate the monks' by daily praying the prayer, "O God, come to my assistance, O Lord, make haste to help me." This is an especially powerful prayer in times of temptation and trial, calling upon God to help us in our need. Or we could take up the "sword of the spirit," the Bible, and immerse ourselves in it, recognizing the "good news" that it contains. Whatever we do, it must be intentional and directed towards the heights of Heaven, realizing that God has destined us to be sons and daughters of light.

"But you, brethren, are not in darkness, that that day should overtake you as a thief. For all you are the children of light, and children of the day: we are not of the night, nor of darkness. Therefore, let us not sleep, as others do; but let us watch, and be sober. For they that sleep, sleep in the night; and they that are drunk, are drunk in the night. But let us, who are of the day, be sober, having on the breastplate of faith and charity, and for a helmet the hope of salvation." (1 Thessalonians 5:4-8)

The spiritual legacy of the last monks of Skellig Michael endures to this day. Let us take it up and continue it, going to the source of their strength, so that we might be able to inspire others by being a light, a city set on a s*kellig* for all to see.

"You are the light of the world. A city seated on a mountain cannot be hid. Neither do men light a candle and put it under a bushel, but upon a candlestick, that it may shine to all that are in the house. So let your light shine before men, that they may see your good works, and glorify your Father who is in heaven." (Matthew 5:14-16)

THE WAY OF THE CROSS, SCELIG MHICHIL.

APPENDIX

PRAYERS & FEAST DAYS

The monks on Skellig Michael would have observed various feast days on the island that recognized their spiritual heritage. Here are a few of the days on the liturgical calendar that they may have celebrated, in addition to the major feasts of the Catholic Church.

January 17 – St. Anthony the Great
February 1 – St. Brigid (Patron of Ireland)
March 17 – St. Patrick (Apostle of Ireland)
April 5 – St. Patrick begins his apostolate in Ireland
April 28 – Suibni in Scelig (Holy monk who died on Skellig)
May 16 – St. Brendan (Patron of County Kerry)
June 9 – St. Columbkille (Patron of Ireland)
September 29 – St. Michael the Archangel
December 12 – St. Finnian of Clonard (Possible Founder of Skellig Michael)

BREASTPLATE OF SAINT PATRICK

This translation is from 1911 and is a literal translation of the original text. It is said that Saint Patrick wrote this prayer during the 5th century.

I bind to myself today
The strong virtue of the Invocation of the Trinity:
I believe the Trinity in the Unity
The Creator of the Universe.

I bind to myself today
The virtue of the Incarnation of Christ with His Baptism,
The virtue of His crucifixion with His burial,

The virtue of His Resurrection with His Ascension,
The virtue of His coming on the Judgement Day.

I bind to myself today
The virtue of the love of seraphim,
In the obedience of angels,
In the hope of resurrection unto reward,
In prayers of Patriarchs,
In predictions of Prophets,
In preaching of Apostles,
In faith of Confessors,
In purity of holy Virgins,
In deeds of righteous men.

I bind to myself today
The power of Heaven,
The light of the sun,
The brightness of the moon,
The splendour of fire,
The flashing of lightning,
The swiftness of wind,
The depth of sea,
The stability of earth,
The compactness of rocks.

I bind to myself today
God's Power to guide me,
God's Might to uphold me,
God's Wisdom to teach me,
God's Eye to watch over me,
God's Ear to hear me,
God's Word to give me speech,
God's Hand to guide me,
God's Way to lie before me,
God's Shield to shelter me,
God's Host to secure me,

Against the snares of demons,
Against the seductions of vices,
Against the lusts of nature,
Against everyone who meditates injury to me,
Whether far or near,
Whether few or with many.

I invoke today all these virtues
Against every hostile merciless power
Which may assail my body and my soul,
Against the incantations of false prophets,
Against the black laws of heathenism,
Against the false laws of heresy,
Against the deceits of idolatry,
Against the spells of witches, smiths, and wizards,
Against every knowledge that binds the soul of man.
Christ, protect me today
Against every poison, against burning,
Against drowning, against death-wound,
That I may receive abundant reward.

Christ with me, Christ before me,
Christ behind me, Christ within me,
Christ beneath me, Christ above me,
Christ at my right, Christ at my left,
Christ in the fort,
Christ in the chariot seat,
Christ in the heart of everyone who thinks of me,
Christ in the mouth of everyone who speaks to me,
Christ in every eye that sees me,
Christ in every ear that hears me.

I bind to myself today
The strong virtue of an invocation of the Trinity,
I believe the Trinity in the Unity
The Creator of the Universe.

IRISH LITANY TO THE
BLESSED VIRGIN MARY

This litany may have been written at the monastery of Clonsast in Ireland around the year 725. It is one of the oldest litanies to the Blessed Virgin Mary. Below is an English translation.

O Great Mary, [*pray for us*]
Mary, greatest of Marys,
Most great of women,
Queen of the angels,
Mistress of the heavens,
Woman full and replete with the grace of the Holy Spirit,
Blessed and most blessed,
Mother of eternal glory,
Mother of the heavenly and earthly Church,
Mother of love and indulgence,
Mother of the golden light,
Honor of the sky,
Harbinger of peace.
Gate of heaven,
Golden casket,
Couch of love and mercy,
Temple of the Divinity,
Beauty of virgins,
Mistress of the tribes,
Fountain of the gardens,
Cleansing of sins,
Washing of souls,
Mother of orphans,
Breast of the infants,
Refuge of the wretched,
Star of the sea,
Handmaid of God,

Mother of Christ,
Abode of the Godhead,
Graceful as the dove,
Serene like the moon,
Resplendent like the sun,
Destruction of Eve s disgrace,
Regeneration of life,
Perfection of women,
Chief of the virgins,
Garden enclosed,
Fountain sealed,
Mother of God,
Perpetual Virgin,
Holy Virgin,
Prudent Virgin,
Serene Virgin,
Chaste Virgin,
Temple of the Living God,
Throne of the Eternal King,
Sanctuary of the Holy Spirit,
Virgin of the root of Jesse,
Cedar of Mount Lebanon,
Cypress of Mount Sion,
Crimson rose in the land of Jacob,
Fruitful like the olive,
Blooming like the palm,
Glorious son-bearer,
Light of Nazareth,
Glory of Jerusalem,
Beauty of the world,
Noblest born of the Christian people,
Queen of life,
Ladder of Heaven,

Hear the petition of the poor; spurn not the wounds and the groans of the miserable.

Let our devotion and our sighs be carried through thee to the presence of the Creator, for we are not ourselves worthy of being heard because of our evil deserts.

O powerful Mistress of heaven and earth, wipe out our trespasses and our sins.

Destroy our wickedness and depravity. Raise the fallen, the debilitated, and the fettered. Loose the condemned. Repair through thyself the transgressions of our immorality and our vices. Bestow upon us through thyself the blossoms and ornaments of good actions and virtues. Appease for us the Judge by thy prayers and thy supplications. Allow us not, for mercy s sake, to be carried off from thee among the spoils of our enemies. Allow not our souls to be condemned, but take us to thyself forever under thy protection.

We, moreover, beseech and pray thee, holy Mary, to obtain, through thy potent supplication, before thy only Son, that is, Jesus Christ, the son of the living God, that God may defend us from all straits and temptations. Obtain also for us from the God of Creation the forgiveness and remission of all our sins and trespasses, and that we may receive from Him further, through thy intercession, the everlasting habitation of the heavenly kingdom, through all eternity, in the presence of the saints and the saintly virgins of the world; which may we deserve, may we enjoy, for ever and ever. Amen

THE SOUL'S DESIRE

An anonymous poem from the 11th century, translated into English by Eleanor Hull.

It were my soul's desire
To see the face of God;
It were my soul's desire
To rest in His abode.

It were my soul's desire
To study zealously;
This, too, my soul's desire,
A clear rule set for me.

It were my soul's desire
A spirit free from gloom;
It were my soul's desire
New life beyond the Doom.

It were my soul's desire
To shun the chills of Hell;
Yet more my soul's desire
Within His house to dwell.

It were my soul's desire
To imitate my King,
It were my soul's desire
His ceaseless praise to sing.

It were my soul's desire
When heaven's gate is won
To find my soul's desire
Clear shining like the sun.

Grant, Lord, my soul's desire,
Deep waves of cleansing sighs;
Grant, Lord, my soul's desire
From earthly cares to rise.

This still my soul's desire
Whatever life afford,
To gain my soul's desire
And see Thy face, O Lord.

BIBLIOGRAPHY

"Skellig Michael." World Heritage Ireland. Accessed April 24, 2017. http://www.worldheritageireland.ie/skellig-michael/built-heritage/the-monastery/.

Archaeologia cambrensis. Vol. IX. 5th. London:Cambrian Archaeological Association, 1892

Gallagher, Timothy M. *Praying the liturgy of the hours: a personal journey.* New York: Crossroad, 2014.

Jungmann, Joseph A. *The Mass of the Roman Rite.* Translated by Francis A. Brunner. Notre Dame: Christian Classics, 2012.

Lavelle, Des, and Des Lavelle. *The Skellig Story: ancient monastic outpost.* Dublin: O'Brien Press, 2004.

Maines, Clark, Walter Horn, Jenny White Marshall, and Grellan D. Rourke. "The Forgotten Hermitage of Skellig Michael." American Journal of Archaeology 95, no. 4 (1991): 758. http://ark.cdlib.org/ark:/13030/ft1d5nb0gb/.

McNamara, Denis R., and Denis R. McNamara. *How to read churches: a crash course in ecclesiastical architecture.* New York: Rizzoli, 2011.

Moorhouse, Geoffrey. *Sun dancing: a vision of medieval Ireland.* New York: Harcourt Brace, 1999.

Noonan, James-Charles. *The church visible: the ceremonial life and protocol of the Roman Catholic Church*. New York: Sterling Ethos, 2012.

Rinzler, J. W. *The Making of Star Wars*. New York: Del Rey Books, 2007.

Stokes, Margaret. *Early Christian architecture in Ireland*. London: G. Bell and Sons, 1878.

Taylor, Chris.*How Star Wars conquered the universe: The past, present, and future of a multibillion dollar franchise*. New York: Basic Books, 2015.

[i] Discover Ireland, "Star Wars The Force Awakens Exclusive: Behind the Scenes with JJ Abrams in Ireland". YouTube video, 1:58. Posted [January 4, 2016]. https://youtu.be/HjnGRTATRdg.

[ii] Ibid.

[iii] Discover Ireland, "Star Wars: The Force Awakens – Behind the Scenes in Ireland". YouTube video, 1:08. Posted [April 15, 2016]. https://youtu.be/i9f2y4jUYq8.

[iv] Hahn, Lucinda. "Spoiler Alert: This Island Appears in 'Star Wars'". *New York Times*, December 1, 2015, Accessed April 22, 2017, https://www.nytimes.com/2015/12/06/travel/star-wars-ireland-skellig-michael.html?_r=0.

[v] Rinzler, J. W. The Making of Star Wars. New York: Del Rey Books, 2007, (Kindle Location 534).

[vi] Klein, Christopher. "The Real History That Inspired "Star Wars". *History,* December 17, 2015, Accessed April 22, 2017, http://www.history.com/news/the-real-history-that-inspired-star-wars.

[viii] Rinzler, (Kindle Location 847).

[viiii] Taylor, Chris.*How Star Wars Conquered the Universe: The Past, Present, and Future of a Multibillion Dollar Franchise.* New York: Basic Books, 2015, .60.

[ix] Pius XII, "On Bees." Translated by Augustine Klaas, S.J. *EWTN,* Accessed April 22, 2017, http://www.ewtn.com/library/papaldoc/p12bees.htm.

[x] Schulte, Augustin Joseph. "Altar Candles." The Catholic Encyclopedia. Vol. 1. New York: Robert Appleton Company, 1907. Accessed April 16, 2017, http://www.newadvent.org/cathen/01347a.htm.

[xi] Jungmann, Joseph A. *The Mass of the Roman Rite.* Translated by Francis A. Brunner. Notre Dame: Christian Classics, 2012, 254.

[xii] McNamara, Denis R. *How to Read Churches.* East Sussex: Ivy Press Limited, 2011, 90.

[xiii] Gallagher, Timothy. *Praying the Liturgy of the Hours: A Personal Journey.* New York: Crossroad Publishing Company, 2014, 6.

[xiv] Vatican Radio, "Pope Francis: Satan exists in the 21st century and how we can fight him,"*News.va*, April 11, 2014, Accessed April 22, 2017, http://www.news.va/en/news/pope-francis-satan-exists-in-the-21st-century-and.

[xv] Pope John Paul II, "Visit to the Shrine of St. Michael on May 24, 1987 at Monte Gargano," May 24, 1987, Accessed April 22, 2017, http://opusangelorum.org/catechesis/monte_gargano.html.

Made in the USA
Middletown, DE
28 May 2024

54993394R00044